Tutti Frut

C000052455

KONSTANDINOS MAHONEY

SPM Publications

London

SPM Publications
Unit 136, 113-115 George Lane, South Woodford,
London E18 1AB, United Kingdom
www.spmpublications.com

First published in Great Britain by SPM Publications – an imprint of
Sentinel Writing & Publishing Company in October 2018.

ISBN 978-0-9935035-8-0

Set in Garamond 9 – 16 points

For Simon, Avra, Jack, Dorothea, Theodora & Clare

Other book by Konstandinos Mahoney

Yo-Yo (Oberon)

Preface

I grew up in Fulham near the river Thames; for many years I had a recurring dream that it was rising, flooding our house, swirling me away in my single bed. Many rivers start off in the mountains, the Ganges, in the Himalayas, The Amazon, in the Peruvian Andes; the Thames bubbles out of a hole in a flat boggy field by an old ash tree in Gloucestershire; when I went to visit it, just like the bear, I found it was dry, only a stone with a worn engraving stating this was the source of the mighty river. Even this is disputed, with some saying the true source is in a mead several miles on – nothing is certain.

The poems in this book bubbled up from somewhere, when I try to trace the flow back to its origin, I get lost - it's confusing to set out in search of something that isn't there. Instinct tells me, close to the source are: my Greek mother's colourful oral histories, her effortless storytelling, use of simile, metaphor, personification, alliteration; the socialist twinkle in my London-Irish father's eyes, the friends and lovers who I've talked, laughed and drank with, the countries and continents I've lived and worked in, the oblique take on life being an outsider has lent me.

You'll see some or all of the above inside the pages of this, my first collection -*Tutti Frutti*.

Acknowledgements

Some poems in this collection have been previously published in UK and international magazines, anthologies and websites, notably:
The Poetry Society website, RAUM, Live Canon, Write To Be Counted, New Writing 6 - Arts Council Anthology, Iron Press, Orbis, and Envoi. (See detailed credits on page 76)

Thanks for support and feedback to: Simon Wu, Trudy Howson, Chris Hardy, Steve Halliwell, Page Kerry Richards, Jennifer Ng, Kavita Jindal and my fellow poets at Barnes and Chiswick Stanza. Special thanks to Roger Elkin for choosing *Tutti Frutti* as a prize winner in the Sentinel Poetry Book Competition and my editor, Nnorom Azuonye.

Contents

TUTTI FRUTTI

Tutti Frutti

We play her records,
big brittle discs slid out with a hiss,
"Tutti frutti, oh rutti"

piano pounding, singer bawling
they jive by the cooker,
dad reading the paper,

mum spinning like a top,
"Wop bop a loo bop a lop ba ba!"
I'd know now, immediately,

Cliff quiff, polo neck, slacks, black,
legs spread, two-tone brogues,
cigarette held backwards.

They dress mannequins,
full skirts, pinched waists, wide-brimmed hats,
elbow length gloves, elegance,

attitude, allure, deities
hovering above the pavement,
living dolls.

Home from school, I barge in
on their afternoon off,
in bed, sun shining in stripes

on naked duplicated breasts.
And when they come down,
she spins a Little Richard, jives with little me.

Riri

We pass him in the street,
silk scarf, blue-rinse, cream trousers,
swirl of cologne in his wake.
She gives my hand a secret squeeze,
'Riri' she sneers, a name they call them
back home, where it all began.

Centre court, men thwacking balls,
calves and thighs flexing as they
crouch and spring. 'Looking at their legs,'
she hisses. I boil with shame. Then see him
sitting on a bench, striped blazer, pooch,
panama – Riri.

Geometry

The blackboard is abstracted with equations.
On the desk - protractors, dividers.

I glance sideways at him,
try to measure the angle between us.

In white linen aprons,
I eye him craftily across the workbench

as we plane wood, releasing the heady scent of resin.
I scatter curly shavings over him.

In break time, beyond the playing fields,
We build a fire; twigs and branches spit and cackle.

He shimmers behind a veil of heat.
In double Biology, we sit together in the lab,

smelling of smoke and desire.
.

An Evening with The Reverend Doctor

Whisky in hand, he pan-fries steaks, singing,
"All creatures that on earth do dwell"
to a young colleague over for a quiet evening,
when an aerosol sweating in the grate, explodes,
lighting up the parlour like a papist grotto.

Later, between sips of malt
he advises the young colleague to fix his foot,
read 'Maurice', 'Palgrave's Golden Treasury,'
buy a set of silver cutlery, spend Easter in Ulster,
stay with his mother in Limavady.
Recalls tumbling down stairs with a Belfast bard,
seeing Michael MacLiammoir play Wilde at the Gate.
Tells how he moved to London to find himself,
how he was beaten for his brogue,
how loneliness skewered his heart,
how comely the young colleague is,
how like a curly-headed Ganymede,
how empty the bottle has become,
how he'll fetch another one.

Recharged, he mounts a chair,
pulls out his member and declares,
"Behold, the mystery, hidden from men's eyes,'
leaps down into a jig, arms stiff at his sides,
hoppin and hollerin till an empty bottle
roasting on the embers cracks like a whip,
and the evening's done. Last train long gone,
the young colleague shares the reverend doctor's bed,
and a night of passionate snoring.

Vampire Madonna

At nine I gave you a valentine - plump red silk heart,
"My love for you burns like a flame in darkness."

Before that were your breasts as you sat on your bed,
deciding for once not to cover up.

Later I killed you off in a dream, your bier drawn
by glossy black horses with purple plumes - I spared no expense.

When I fled north to university, you bombarded me with
food parcels, home baked cakes heavy as guilt.

And when I came down between terms, hiding behind
a mess of long hair, you fed me so that I could hardly move.

Then you wrecked my marriage and completely broken
I came back, and you hunted everyone I loved.

Once, on a Greek island, I saw a woman call her son
from the sea, "Kostaki! Kostaki!"

He waded out, balding, pot-bellied, hair-chested,
and she wrapped him in a towel and led him away.

Aunt Aphrodite

Gum stuck like a boil
between thin-pencilled brows,
she nods, blows smoke, as mum
unlocks the symbols in her dregs;
a different future every seven days.

One wet weekend we go to hers,
a council flat just off the Lillie Road.
She shows us a message from an admiral
written in pencil on a gilt-edged menu,
thanking her for services rendered;
black and white photos in silver frames;
her and Uncle Bill by the Parthenon;
snapshot of their handsome son,
(breastfed till the age of nine);
her on a beach, in skimpy bikini
with stocky youth in bulging briefs.

Back home from school, mum still at work,
she rings the bell. To pass the time,
suggests a game of hypnotism.
My eyes fixed on her swinging crucifix
trying to ignore her pendulous breasts,
the sticky wetness on my tight-clenched knees.

Mum's silver spoons start disappearing.
"She's stuffing them down her drawers," dad says;
In her defense, I say, "She doesn't wear any."

Maenad

Pianist strikes up.
Nervous of her mother's marble fists,

she sets off tout de suite in triple time,
bourrée, valeta, mazurka, tarantella,

clockwork ballerina,
key grinding in her back.

At a grand house in Kolonaki,
residence of Madam Komnenos,

(descendant of Imperial Byzantines),
she steers her to the centre, announces

the morning's entertainment to ladies
sipping Turkish coffee from gilded demitasses.

Dizzy, she spins too close to the curtains -
a whoosh of darkness buries her.

Back home, door slams, lift clicks and hums.
Locked in she's free to crouch, leap, twist,

bend bars, bring down walls,
crash, laugh, cry, leap up to scratch the sky.

Athena Nike

Overwhelmed by masterpieces,
we shuffle wearily down lengthy galleries,
(she refused point blank to let me hire a wheelchair).

Then we see her, headless, floating in air,
spray-drenched chiton clinging to
epic breasts, Amazonian thighs,

marmoreal wings flaring behind her
skewed by a wind fierce enough to blow
a hero off course for ten full years,

fifty in my mother's case, so long away
the two countries she calls home
each thinking her a foreigner.

Surgical stockings stuck out before her
she stares at the past, conjures Smyrna in flames,
flight to Alexandria, Athens in the occupation, liberation,

civil war, an English soldier, love, London, me,
gifting our story the ancient way,
there beneath Victory's beating wings.

Sideline

In this game there's someone to blow the whistle,
call a halt if things get out of hand,
won't always be, so run boys, run,
chase that ball and if you catch it,
clutch its oval tight against your heart.

The fathers, pale legs, baggy shorts,
bellies curving under polo shirts,
bellow as their offspring charge past.
What a mess they've made of things,
how they long for their boys to make a better stab.

Cheers, applause, the final whistle blows;
they invade the pitch, congratulate, console,
linger, chatting as the boys get changed,
then carry off their cubs in cars
reliving the match as if it were their own.

Dormition *

Gently lowering his hands

she floats suspended
between earth and sky,
a conjuror's assistant,

a lifetime of
clinging to the shore,
over.

Stunned by the mid-August sun,
weak from fasting,
she let him coax her in

right up to her breasts,
tilt her gently sideways
off her feet,

rests her vertical,
on his fingertips.

Glittering sea pup,
the son swims under her,
looks up at the keel of her back,

arms open like wings,
down at the rippling crucifix
of her shadow.

Eyes closed, face framed
by a blinding halo,
she is ready.

From the shore drifts
a pulsing chant of cicadas,
the fragrant scent of pine.

In Greek Orthodoxy, The Dormition of the Theotokos, August 15th celebrates the 'falling asleep' of the Virgin Mary and her bodily resurrection before being taken up to heaven

Passing the Ball

Eight sharp, Sunday mornings,
I stand, spick and span by
tight tucked bed, hospital corners,
buffed shoes.

Stiff-backed, clipped tache he comes
reeking of bay rum, inspects fold of sheet,
shine of shoe, checks under bed
for presence of dust.

One Sunday, no show.
At breakfast, stares at egg and bacon.
Asked what's wrong, says he's had a dream,
(shocked to learn he has such things as dreams)

they're hiding behind dunes,
waiting for a lull to swim out to boats
moored offshore. They make a dash,
a shell explodes, his best mate's head

goes flying through the air,
"like a football," he says.
That night, a ball lands at my feet,
looks up wide-eyed, tries to speak.

Curfew

Head spinning with hormones and booze,
snogged mouth tingling,

cheeks glowing with beard-burn,
late home, he creeps up unlit stairs.

A floorboard groans - geese of Rome.
Freezes.

Heart pounds.
Fridge purrs.

A flash of striped pyjamas,
knuckles crack his face.

As the boy wreaks his room,
IT'S HIS FATHER'S FACE HE'S SMASHING IN!

Mutiny

Gesturing, bellows
'IN!'
'NOW!'

Treading water,
the boy eyes him,
voice, body, authority,

shrunk by distance,
monkey man
on the warpath again,

hoo hoo hoo.
He swivels round
to face the open sea.

Piano Practice

Notes perch thick as starlings on telegraph wires,
the key is a complex density of grids,
Mozart, pop-eyed, precocious,
is making mules of the boy's lumpy hands.

Stamping hard on the forte pedal,
he hurls his vengeful fists
down into the very teeth of it,
gorging on a sumptuous thunder roll.

Gathering silence leaves the metronome
wagging a finger and clicking its tongue
in a mischievous fraction of time.

Airborne

"Mountains" "Clouds"
"Mountains" "CLOUDS!"

In a gap between the seats in front,
Dad's face appears. "It's the Alps."

"Told you!" she goes.
"And clouds." I poke out my tongue.

A lady pushing a pram pulls up,
gives away drinks in cans, little bottles.

Somewhere over Yugoslavia,
Dad's face appears again,

"Know what?" he says, smiling dreamily,
"Wouldn't mind if we went down, right now, together."

Plane lands unexpectedly to scattered screams,
careens along the runway

engines roaring in reverse.
When it stops, there's applause.

We step out into burning sunshine,
the smell of oil, heat, pine;

bounce down rickety metal steps
to another world.

In the crowded shuttle bus,
holding mum's hand,

I look up at him.
Is this what he wanted?

.

The Consolation of Art

We set off somewhere in the Middle Ages,
up the royal road of art,
dying father in a wheelchair.

On either side, crucified Christs
twist this way and that,
in postures of serene agony.

We pause, Mid-Victorian, a massive Martin,
rivers of volcanic lava, cascading boulders,
seismic chasm, bishops, courtiers, kings

plunging headlong into hell;
he stares up at the cinematic cataclysm
with what I hope is socialist satisfaction.

Mid-Twentieth, a blindfold fist-head
on long straining neck, bared vicious teeth;
a pontiff strapped to an electric chair

screams as we hurry past. Gratefully, I wheel him
into the gift shop, art tamed, copied and for sale,
buy him a print of a dissolving sunrise; then take him home.

Death of Poseidon

He looks down at stork legs,
pebble toes, his manhood, a whelk
peeping through suds -
he has become the dying father
he once bathed, soaped down
with ginger tenderness.

At ease with nakedness,
the daughter bathes him,
chatters, makes him smile,
swaddles his gaunt frame
in soft white cotton,
towels him dry.

Holed up in his room, the son,
too scared to get close,
to look upon an iron god in rust,
wary of unknotted tongues,
the crippled tenderness
that still might show.

Swan Song

Swamped in Christmas jumper,
trousers baggy even on first notch,
he makes his way downstairs.

Tissue crown on bony head,
he sits with offspring around a golden bird
gifted from his never-ending store.

Sherry dabbed on cracked lips,
in reedy treble breaks into song,
"I do like to be beside the seaside."

"Tiddly-om-pom-pom!" they singalong;
segues into Danny Boy, "the pipes, the pipes..."
Spent, slowly mounts the stairs, never to come down,

with breath in him, again.

Sugar Babe

The Sugababes are serenading
patients on the dementia ward.

"And my knees are weak
And my mouth can't speak
Fell too far this time."

Three beds down,
curled up around her final days,
Aunt May, the wild one,

always up for a lark,
love child with a G.I. -
now due to be unplugged.

"Cos I'm slipping away
Like the sand to the tide."

I lightly stroke her brittle hair,
softly coo her name.

"Too lost in you, lost in you."

Eyes fidget under lids,
a throaty grunt.

"If you get too near
I might disappear
I might lose my mind."

Farewell Auntie,
my good time girl,
my sugar babe.

Songbird Rides the MTR

Held out before him like a paper lantern,
the old man takes his covered cage
down a flow of metal stairs
to the underworld.

Nerve on a perch, the leiothrix,
red bill glued shut, seed heart bursting,
in a metallic roar is rushed along
granite bore holes beneath Hong Kong.

Rising up, the man exits the station,
strolls to a nearby park, unveils the wooden cage,
hangs it from a branch of an osmanthus tree.
The tiny troubadour twitches into life,

its pent up silvery song trilling through bars,
scaling up past banks of grumbling air-conditioners
to where raptors soar on towering updrafts.

Aberdeen Street

Climbing the steep gradient of his street
from harbour side to half way up the hill,
a merchant seaman, short and wiry,
swag bag lumpy with gifts for wife and son.
He crosses tramlines, passes stalls loaded
with pomelo, pak choi, bitter melon;
shops stocked with jars of fungi, penis,
horn; the spiky salt tang of dried fish
following him like the call of the sea,
till finally, up creaking flights of stairs
he rises to the curtained space of home.

On his bunk bed, face to the wall,
he hears his father make those noises,
mother creeping off to wash herself.
He pings the plane's propellers,
rubs the metal key, the stiffness
in his shorts; smells the rank odour
of body waste as the fragrant ladies
creep in at dawn to empty
night soil from kitchen bins.

The tin plane growls across the floor.
One day it will be his turn to leave,
soar over the port, while his father
sits at home staring through
flickering glass.

Year of the Ox

Many moons after I'd swapped hearts
with their son, we meet in their tiny
tower block flat on the third day
of the Lunar New Year.

The round table we sit at fills
the entire space he grew up in.
His mother chats in Cantonese,
father stirs an iron wok.

Dishes land in a rush,
mapo tofu, butterfly prawns,
crispy beef, boiled rice;
chopsticks spring, feast begins.

Sipping Johnny Walker,
I leaf through his logbook,
Shanghai, Rio, Cape Town,
London, Hamburg, Rotterdam.

And there it ends,
something must have shown,
the way I looked at their son,
was too much at home.

New Lucky House

Porter's head buried in the racing pages,
anyone can slip in, flit soundlessly across
soggy cardboard, share the lift with bearded

giant in salwar kamiz, petite Filipina,
her bodyweight in stripy canvas bags,
youth with headphones leaking cantopop,

tattooed tough in shorts and singlet,
grey-haired westerner with samsonite –
what's he doing in this seedy ziggurat

back turned on downtown smart hotels?
Naked on a narrow pallet, New Lucky House,
he lies wide-eyed, eight hours behind,

watches neon pulsing on the ceiling,
listens to the air-conditioner's tantric hum.
He's done with mountains, markets, museums,

with souvenirs, novelties, nightlife, sin.
What's he searching for? Running from?
Taking home nothing but the need to leave again.

Heavenly Turtle

Beside a crowded port - junks,
floating restaurants, cargo ships -

a mass of black volcanic rock rises,
terraced tombs ascending in tiers.

Photographs on gravestones show
faces smiling out to sea;

now tower blocks intrude, break the chi,
the vital link of land and water.

The stone ball in the lion's mouth
is seldom turned, stone steps become

too steep for those with memories to climb.
A Hakka woman in black-fringed hat,

sweeps neglected paths; curved turtle back,
the sky resting on her carapace.

Night Market

An ambush of darkness,
night falls sudden on Louang Phrabang,

Market stalls light up the length of Sisavangvong:
Hmong blankets, bags, Buddhas, Soviet flags,

brassware puppets, T-shirts, leather belts,
antiques, made in China, going for a song,

pay in crumpled kip, or dollar.
Market's end, he walks past waiting tuk tuks,

strolls down unlit country road,
fields sown with coffee, rice, beans, bombs,

sloping down to the dark Mekong,
patrolled by giant rays, flesh-eating catfish.

Mosquitos hum and whine, a soft voice purrs,
"Girl sir, want girl? Young girl? Boy sir? Opium?"

Negros

A naked bulb defines the shoreline
of his rum-gold body sprawled
on the white cotton sheet.

Resting flat on the silk of his chest,
a silver crucifix glints daggers at me.
His smile is slow, wide, unrefined -

he is Negros,
my sugar island,
my sudden friend.

Somehow he shapes a story,
how on the slopes of Canlaon Vulcan
men sleep wrapped around guns,

snakes coiled around cane,
dreaming of taking back the sweetness
of their land.

Ladyboy

A woman's face and form, bar one small detail,
smooth-legged she strides along the Silom Soi,
allure and pulling power never failing,
my Bangkok belle, my beau, my ladyboy.
Her painted face can trick the reeling sailor,
catch husband tourist poet unaware,
together stagger from the Pat Pong parlour,
and through the back door mount the groaning stairs.
She lip-synchs Whitney at the Colosseum,
the songs she sings to me are out of tune,
but being so, are sweet, so carpe-diem,
in nature's off-key love notes let us croon.
With ying and yang together for good measure,
The him in her and her in him my treasure.

Andros

Flat chests tanned tawny gold,
they gaze in agony through misted glass

at tubs of coloured creams - strawberry,
mint, peach.

Cones cross the counter,
tongues nudge into numbing sweetness.

Outside, a hoplite in shining armour,
waits to march them across the island

to where a wooden ship is moored
ready to sail.

In a closed circle
they linger in the air-conditioning,

exchanging looks
as they kiss away their melting scoops.

Immortals

They sprint with splashing ankle wings,
leap hurdle lines of crumbling waves,
dive, silver streaming from their lips,
rise laughing, gasping, gulping air,
mount sparkling on each other's backs.

In knotted crown, gaunt arms raised
above the swell, an ancient monarch stands
on shifting sands, the pull of tide against his shanks.
At the far end - rocks, a set of caprine teeth,
flossed by an indifferent wind.

Macedonian Gold

Inside, beyond the turnstiles, behind glass, is the gold,
figures that dance around a glistening urn,
genitals and breasts raised from the tomb.

A golden wreathe floats weightlessly in space,
supreme confidence, indifference,
its delicate leaves trembling in the air-conditioning.

Outside, summer's furnace, stink of the bay,
an armed guard in his sentry box,
strays sleeping in his shadow.

A teacher stands on the entrance steps,
gestures to his assembled students,
voice raised against traffic and indifference.

He strives to inspire them,
to raise them up to the gold (that doesn't care).
to extract them from the present, (their bodies).

Sunlight settles on their shoulders in golden epaulettes,
burns holes in his authority,
he barely holds them, save a few in the front.

He claps his hands, they slowly shuffle forward,
sunlight slipping off their shoulders
as, one by one, they step inside.

The Alexandrian*

Round spectacles, dapper suit and tie,
portfolio tucked primly underarm,
from Rue Lepsius he makes his way,
past brothel, church and hospital,
a clerk en route to his ministry,
the Water Board, his satrapy,
Third Circle of Irrigation,
British colonial administration,
the daily grind, the Archimedean screw,
and in return, his monthly due.

At night he cruises Boulevard Ramelah,
pick ups in the Souk Al-Attarine,
hook ups at The Café al Salam,
payment in Egyptian pounds,
sex with sailors, waiters, stevadores,
muscled torsos, alabaster,
ideal bodies, olive skin,
mechanic's grease, sweet jasmine,
salt tasting kisses, aniseed,
fulfilling deep dark secret needs.

Careless of fame and publication,
ducking censure and tradition,
without fuss, shame, inhibition,
abandons English, convention, rhyme,
writes free iambic, classic, demotic,
Hellenic, syllabic, homoerotic,
passes, to a few discerning friends,
hand-written poems fastened with a pin,
history made flesh, memory revived,
a marble korus opens living eyes.

Rich with all he's gained along the way,
a line of burnt out candles in his wake,
cancer grabs him by the throat,
on the same day he was born, he dies,
leaves the body, and the work,

reminding us, and all who follow,
to make our journey brave and long,
full of passion and instruction,
free of guilt and inner demons,
undeterred by angry Poseidon.

*Constantine Cavafy (1863-1933)

Night Train to Prague

The wagon-lit a racing catacomb -
stacked stiffly in our narrow tiers,
passports nestling near our hearts,
forced to sleep by an iron lullaby.

Along the corridor a yoghurt seller calls,
curdled milk, wise wrinkled skin,
a nursery of baby faces,
cluster of moons.

He calls out to his sleeping customers,
to the stone angels of a deaf city,
gargoyles vomiting ice,
cold deserted squares.

Praha

As you step out
into the crowded, cobbled streets,
someone's waiting for you,
someone you do not know,
some ordinary Joe or Josef
who bumps into you,
apologizes, moves on.

When later you discover your loss,
behind the dismay
steals a feeling of enlightenment,
your passport and wallet swapped
for anonymity, the mendicant's bowl.

You can't recall the exact moment
you were singled out,
but it's close to the time the Staré Město
with its bohemian charm, stole your heart.
Now, unencumbered, you are more truly
a stranger, free to discover
who you want to be.

Chasing the Fall

It's a bad year for leaves; the guidebook's cover
shows New England painted scarlet, amber, gold.
But as we drive Upstate, the trees are
stubborn green, mawkish yellow.

We cross into Canada, hoping,
as temperatures dip, colours will rise.
In Montreal our hostess gives a Gallic shrug, '
This year no good for feuillage."

In the fuzz of Vermont dusk,
a doe takes shape. Brake too late.
Get out to a bashed-in bonnet,
Empty road, the shakes.

New Hampshire, Massachusetts drift by -
rain-blurred vistas, mist covered summits,
leafless valleys, vacant lakes. At Portsmouth,
a milky sea fog rolls in shutting everything down.

Bloomsbury Set

Georgian terraces line up either side,
a guard of honour standing to attention,
blue plaques, medals pinned to uniforms;
the meter's clocking up a king's ransom;
a lifetime in the forces overseas,
he's coming home in style.

Outside a handsome red brick mansion
youths idle on the entrance steps,
eye the luggage lining up below them,
sniff the leather, note the tip,
observe the cabbie's whispered warning,
the dapper man, suitcase in hand,
looking through them to the door behind.

Up

No flowing cape,
no arms out straight,
vertical you rise and flow
looking down past feet
at white cliffs fringed
with sea, a patchwork
of green gold fields
extending into haze,
up at a big bare sky
curved like the cornea
of god's eye.

Sometimes take off
fails, the conscious wish
a spanner in the works.
You have to be abandoned
to rise and fly.

Monday

Sunday night, he lies in bed, a small letter i,
Monday is a big problem,
the night sky a vast blackboard,
there are no stars in his maths book.

The television mumbles on downstairs
till God Save the Queen shuts down the house.
Outside the bare trees thrash thrash their canes,
the wind bends over and howls.

Hauled through long slow streets,
stilled in rows and registered,
Miss writes up the date
with a shrieking stick of chalk.

Granny's Ghost

In the downstairs bedroom
Grannys' resting in her coffin,

a big cracked doll
embalmed in moonlight.

Upstairs, mum and dad,
mackerel stilled in starlight.

Under golden eiderdown
sister curled up like a prawn.

Stiff as a drowned tin soldier,
I lie awake, listening.

Suddenly I pick up
the light tread of granny on the stairs,

risen
for the final supernatural nag.

The child is up,
flashing across the hall

to hack the mackerel
from their ice packs.

The Reader

The room is a puffball of dust,
a loaf turns powder blue,
a pilgrimage of ants winds to a pagoda
of unwashed dishes.

Absent landlord, the reader sits
rocked to stillness by the rhythm
of his book, his head, a wave born keg,
bobbing every time he turns a page.

Cherry Orchard

Last night the bare arthritic trees
bent over black ice-blistered sticks
and harried by a dog-toothed wind
hobbled down a flint edged cliff.

At dawn, they stood against the sky
all spattered in a petalled froth
come sudden as ecstatic foam
that blooms on epileptic lips.

Beeze

Bright as soft chips off a tiger's back they roll
leaving a long trail of falling zzzz's
as in comic books when someone sleeps.

Can throw a big room into panic
swinging through a window with disproportionate noise.
They tickle the fearless face of flowers,

explore the foxgloves' bugle tubes,
land boldly on the face of sunflowers,
gathering gold dust in their ankle baskets.

Now they are being put away for winter,
picked out of nature with invisible tweezers
as the flowers wrinkle and lose their hair.

Fox

The fox and moon break cover from bush and cloud,
cold and hard the mineral planet and the purpose.
The moon has a bite of darkness in its neck,
Reynard is a Gladstone bag of greed.

The hens bunch, pushing up their fat breasts together,
the cock seems a puny warrior now,
colours on his throat wringing his neck,
his crow cracking like an old scratched disc.

The hens begin their low crazy talk.
Red as lipstick he comes,
chicken wire soft as a bridal veil;
leaves with a vast bloom in his mouth.

He leaps into sheep as if they were clouds,
pouring himself tooth and nail into their vaguery,
dispersing them like smoke with the wind of his rush,
a furious snowstorm of wool,

the fox spinning in it like a Catherine Wheel.

Togo

The buried street glares with snow.
In the polar brilliance

I squint at my gloveful of envelopes,
matching their smudged arithmetic

with numbers on doors.
A stamp, Togo, tropical bird

bright as blood,
melts a hole in my frosted eye.

I fold and poke the large stiff card
through the door's tight jaw,

hear it land with a light matted thump,
the sound a bird might make

fallen frozen from a tree.

Twelfth Night

Stripped bare, peg-legged, balding,
dumped outside as whining vacuums
suck up clattering needles.

Those that threw them out
first waltzed them in,
dressed them in jewels,

draped them in pulsing lights,
crowned them with stars,
stacked gifts at their feet

and with shut eyes inhaled
the resin scent of fairy tale,
concrete melting into gingerbread.

Now, back to work,
shifty former hosts
look the other way

embarrassed by the line of amputees
sprawled along the street,
strands of tarnished tinsel clinging on,

ashamed of the child
that took them in, the adult
that turfed them out.

Child's Painting of a Wedding

The floating groom is anchored to the lawn
by dribbling fingers rooted to the soil,
the bride bagged in a gladiatorial net,
a brood of daisies writhing in her claws,
a fat sun splashes sweat,
his clownish grin a bloodshot U,
a best man belly laugh out of the blue.
Below a mob of black stick wedding guests
with raised prehensile bones,
discharge a festive hail of coloured stones.

Vinegar

They greet him at the airport,
forced smiles, brittle cheer,

hiding the news in case he crashes.
He drags it from them,

drives off chasing the sound barrier
through desert vacancy,

races up past rows of lookalike bungalows
to the one at the top;

steps into a dismembered room;
rushes to the nursery

crammed full of emptiness.

Swing

In a garden
on a hill
metal frame
creaking chains
wide-eyed
stiff-legged
a little girl
swinging
daddy pushing
singing
a swing-song
in grandma's
native sing-song
koon-YA
be-LA
epes-E
kope-LA
she flies from hin
soaring over
roof tops
palm trees
sand
koon-YA
be-LA
slicing back
bolting up
hair flying
toes rising
higher
faster
harder
chains kink
seat twists
smashes back
empty, hard
into his face

Handover

Phoenix,
10 a.m.

They're coming -
he's holding her hand.

She sees me, breaks free.
I catch her, lift her,

feel her little arms
tight around my neck.

"Four sharp," he barks,
and marches, fuming, back to barracks.

Phoenix
4 p.m.

She's dozing in my arms,
a day of fun and laughter.

He strides towards us,
I softly kiss her hair.

He takes her,
twists her round

to face the other way.

Hotel Claire de Lune

Books a hotel, somewhere to go
for the six hours they have together.

An old forgotten maid from number ten
comes stretching out a sweet-filled begging hand -

you biff balloons to her, coloured globes,
that crackle as they graze her woolly clothes.

A deaf boy with a tarter face
gallops through your scattered spread of toys

bugling on a torn reed in his throat -
you lightly touch his hectic cheek,

pick him out a clockwork clown,
disarm him in the name of play.

But down the corridor a crocodile creeps,
a loud legal clock ticking thorough its grinning teeth.

They hurry through the lobby to the hired car,
he fumbles with the child seat's puzzle lock,

goggles at his watch grown dartboard size,
they stare at each other with saucer eyes.

He drives back bawling nursery rhymes,
windscreen-wipers beating frantic time.

On the dot, pull up outside the mother's door
that slams shut on her tiny baffled face.

Six Hundred

Cradled in his arm, she suckles on
a soft rubber teat, the warm formula
he upends for her.

Words sprout in her mouth like milk teeth,
vowels, consonants lego-lock -
ma-ma, da-da.

Letting go of a chair,
she sprints across the rug
into his open arms.

They chat in tenor, piping treble,
questions, stories, funny noises,
sing wobbly duets.

On a slippery tea tray
he skims her across the lawn,
crickets leaping either side like dolphins.

High on eucalyptus leaves
a camel peers across the garden wall
- they sing and dance for him.

She walks barefoot amongst ants
big enough to have shadows,
with a soft tap releases a bird from the cat's maw.

Outside her memory
those first six hundred days
that for him, are now.

After Access

listless balloons
graze on the rug

animals
stiff on their sides

new doll
flat on her face

bubbles
stains on the floor

an abandoned sandwich
small crescent bite

grinning stickmen
frozen scrawl

Japanese camera
loaded with smiles

spell in a bucket
tipped down the sink

man on sofa
stiff drink

Ring Ring

He knows from the hectoring way
the phone is ringing - it's her.

She speaks with martinet briskness,
a touch of ice – is he talking to the wife?

Fine, thanks, needs money,
food, water, electricity,

last time not enough -
does he want her to starve, stink, freeze?

He agrees.
She's late, has to go, goodbye, thank you.

Is gone.

His Values

Suddenly she's there,
sitting at my kitchen table,
boyfriend at her side,
a woman now,

mother's hair and eyes,
dash of me. At her request
the past is off limits,
no raking up, recrimination,

'tis the season to be jolly,
so, fa la la la la,
let common genes carol.
Supper for three, pop up family,

clay lid floats off steaming casserole,
hasn't tasted daddy's cooking in a while.
I say something wrong,
she starts to cry,

'He gave me my values,' she whimpers,
dabbing moist eyes.
Next morning, they leave -
earlier than planned.

Car turns the corner.
Gone.

Fable

Kidnapped when I was on the wing,
you were taken to a secret lair, plucked,
cased in armour, taught to chew leaves,
lumber on all fours, retract your head
when I approached believing I meant
to carry you off, drop you on rocks,
crack you open.

But look, you too have a beak,
and tucked away inside you
are wings; unpack them,
push them through gaps in your shell,
then flap them hard till you rise,
soaring up to meet your song.

Finishing Line

There, finally, rippling in the heat,
scaffold arch, sponsor's logo - the finishing line.
Running on empty, cupboard bare,

somehow something not there, is there;
he's going to have a go, make a show,
might even manage a little wave,

plucky die-hard, last and proud.
But where is everyone, the cheering crowd,
officials with clipboards, bottles of water?

Hasn't seen a living soul since that ostrich
overtook him on the hanging bridge.
Blood drains, head spins - blackout.

Wakes to fire ants marching past his nose,
a sun-bleached ad for a soft drink
you can no longer buy.

Dr Mirabilis and the Brass Wall That Will Save England

"How," she muses, "do we keep them out?"
"Mirabilis will know," pipes up the fool,
a mop-head jokester swamped in crumpled clothes,
"he's as wizardly in truth as in trickery."
"Go fetch," she charges, crossing leathered legs.
Forth he bumbles, north to distant shires,
home to freckled Vikings
and offspring of the Commonwealth,
finds the alchemist hard at work
transforming foaming pottles into piss.

Brought before her, the magician marvels,
the automaton he has dreamed of making.
Off come his spectacles, the rhetoric rises,
"May a storming Brexit thunder from its cave,
and dim fair Europe to a dark eclipse."
He smiles the way daredevil Drake once did
when busting Spain, or cloaking puddles for his Queen.
"Even if ten Boneys reigned in Brussels,
with all the power they command,
they shall not touch a grass of English ground
for I will circle England round with brass,
a shining wall sprung from your mouth,
command and it shall ring the English strand,
bolder than the slabs that sliced Berlin,
the barricade that stays the Latin tide,
encircling like the mighty ring of Jove
from Dover to the market-place of Rye."
Then speaks The Head, "Sovereignty" it says.
"Et nunc et semper, amen," an owlish friar drones
(while taking selfies for his instagram).
A flash of lightning, Big Ben wakes and booms,
a witch swoops in with a frozen leg of lamb,
 "This meat is not for turning," she declares,
and brings it down hard upon The Head – the wall is dead.

Roger Bacon, popularly known as Doctor Mirabilis, was a thirteenth century English philosopher, alchemist and friar; he believed that he could create a magical, mechanical brass head that could conjure up a brass wall that would encircle England and protect her from European influence and incursion. Elizabethan playwright Richard Greene wrote a comedy about Roger Bacon and his brass head – 'Friar Bacon and Friar Bungay'. Text from Greene's play is the basis of the poem.

Hell's Kitchen

Late home, exhausted,
pig of a day,
zap a lasagne,
pour a rosé,
flop down on sofa,
turn on TV.
Line of men kneeling,
bright orange jumpsuits,
heads bowed, clean-shaven,
white desert sand,
soldiers behind them,
each with a curved blade,
a personal butcher for every man.

Grab the remote,
hop to new channel,
land in a kitchen
all shiny and new,
celebrity chef,
chatty and cheerful
showing you how
to butterfly lamb,
"Run your knife slowly,
like this, down the centre,
then cut through the flesh
to reveal the bone."

Fugitive

At night the scrape of coat hangers.
We pass food through a crack in the door.

We look in the mirror.
How do we dare?

Next morning the wardrobe is open -
inside, the reek of stables.

We muck it out, lay fresh newspaper
that has your face on it.

Gift

If you see us climbing over the wall
into your garden,
do not call the law,
we come with gifts,
not in these ragged bundles,
no frankincense or myrrh in there,
no gold sewn into the lining.

We bring you something else,
something mislaid for so long
you have forgotten what it was.
As you open the door to let us in,
perhaps you will remember
what it was you once lost,
for now it is found.

Pride

In sparkling lurex the trans woman moves forward
on her scooter, pup boys in leather dog masks

strain ahead on leashes, and as we round the corner
a breeze catches our rainbow flags, blows your hand

into mine. The crowds lined up the length of Oxford Street cheer
as man and man we march proud and fearless to Trafalgar Square.

In Whitehall, marshals wave us to a side street.
Parade over we stack banners, take group photos, hug,

say goodbye – the golden lady motors off, handlers unleash
their pups, and as we merge back into the crowds

I notice, we're no longer holding hands.

The One

Overcrowded basement,
bodies crushed against a bar,
we swap smiles;
and in that teeming aviary of tipsy men
shrieking above the boom and thump
of dance anthems, we are drawn into a
stillness so singular that when the lights
go up on a shabby, shrunken dive,
we are still in wonderland, my heart
spinning like a glitter ball and I know
this is the moment, you are the one.

African Icarus

Voice raised against the planes,
"Male, black, early twenties, hoody, jeans,
trainers, mobile phone, tissue in both ears."

We were still in bed as his Boeing
rumbled overhead, heard a terrific bang
and when we looked out,
there he was face down, blind drunk,
is what we first thought till we saw
the blood pumping out from under him.

Young, fit, he might have survived
the starved air in the wheel-well,
the bone-biting cold, been awake
as the undercarriage yawned open
over the broad looping Thames,
Mortlake's labyrinth rushing up
to break him.

Looking for a better life, they said
and he might have found one
had he landed on his feet,
we would have welcomed him,
given him something to eat,
made up the bed in Jamie's old room.

'*Dr Mirabilis and the Brass Wall That Will Save England*' was winner of The Poetry Society Stanza Competition 2017 and is published on the Poetry Society Web Site, along with a poetry video of the poem, at http://poems.poetrysociety.org.uk/poems/dr-mirabilis-and-the-brass-wall-that-will-save-england/.

'*Songbirds Rides the MTR*' was recorded and broadcast at Covent Garden Tube Station throughout National Poetry Day, 2017.

'*Tutti Frutti*' was shortlisted for The Bridport Poetry Competition 2017.

'*An Evening With The Reverend Doctor*' was published by RAUM 2017.

'*The Consolation of Art*' and '*Passing The Ball*' were published in Live Canon Anthologies 2014 & 2017,

'*Ladyboy*' was published in Live Canon's '*154*' an anthology of poetry responding to Shakespeare's sonnets.

'*Twelfth Night*' was published in Live Canon's '*New Poems for Christmas*' Anthology.

'*Pride*' and '*Gift*' were published in '*Write To Be Counted*' an anthology of poetry to uphold human rights, editors, Bulman, Jackson, Jones.

'*Fox*' published in, New Writing 6, Arts Council Anthology, Ed. Ted Hughes.

'*Child's Painting of A Wedding,*' '*Togo,*' '*The Schoolboy,*' '*Piano Practice,*' and '*Cherry Orchard,*' all published by Iron Press.

'*Macedonian Gold*' and '*Night Train to Prague*' published by Orbis.

'*Beeze*' and '*Granny's Ghost*' published in Envoi,

'*Vampire Madonna*' published in Vision On: Michael Johnson Memorial Poetry Competition The background to, '*New Lucky House*' can be read online on my Asia Literary Review blog at http://www.asialiteraryreview.com/new-lucky-house

Lightning Source UK Ltd.
Milton Keynes UK
UKHW01f0608251018
331169UK00001B/71/P